Once there was a traveler.

An artist.

A cosmic, celestial, musical artist who traveled far and wide,
who searched for and discovered
different people, places, and sounds.

Many artists develop a particular sound and style of music.
And once established, that sound and style changes no more.

This traveler was different. Instead of resisting change, he faced change—he embraced change—time and time again. Perhaps you're like this too. Always excited by the search for the new. Always bored by the sameness of the familiar.

From each cosmic journey, this artist took inspiration.
He learned from others and learned about himself.
At every turn, he changed the sound of his music.
He even changed the way he looked.
All in response to each new world explored.

Let's go visit these worlds.
Let's see his transformations.
Facing
embracing
the thrill of change.

This
was
David Bowie.

To Neal—thanks for everything

Neal Porter Books
An imprint of Holiday House Publishing, Inc.
Edited by Taylor Norman

Printed and bound in May 2026 at C&C Offset, Shenzhen, China.
The artwork for this book was created in the same spirit that Bowie created—in lots of different ways.
Pen and ink, watercolor, graphite, collage, ballpoint pen, colored pencil, gouache, and acrylic.
Book design by Matthew Cordell and Jennifer Browne
www.holidayhouse.com
First Edition
1 3 5 7 9 10 8 6 4 2
ISBN: 978-0-8234-5155-5 (hardcover)

Library of Congress Cataloging-in-Publication Data is available.

EU Authorized Representative: HackettFlynn Ltd, 36 Cloch Choirneal,
Balrothery, Co. Dublin, K32 C942, Ireland. EU@walkerpublishinggroup.com

STARMAN

The Cosmic Voyage of David Bowie

MATTHEW CORDELL

NEAL PORTER BOOKS
HOLIDAY HOUSE / NEW YORK

MAJOR TOM

How does it feel to be celebrated for what you like to do?
Does it make you want more of that feeling?
Does it make you want to keep going and work harder?

Bowie lived and breathed music, even as he was just beginning to explore it. Always playing instruments, always singing.
A born performer.
And yet, before he was grown up, he was unsure who he would be or what sort of music he would make.

After a lot of wondering and a little bit of wandering to find the perfect sound and the perfect place, Bowie arrived somewhere that felt right. A spacey place, full of dreams come true and dreams imagined. A place with music that seemed as if it were transmitted from the stars.

And there, Bowie found his sound . . .

As Major Tom.

Dreamy and electronic.

Peaceful strumming of guitar
layered with intergalactic sounds,
and interstellar lyrics.

...5...4...3...2...1...

Bowie launched to success.

And when his journey was over . . .

it wasn't over.

It was only the beginning of his intergalactic discovery.

It was time he faced the change.

ZIGGY STARDUST

Have you ever wondered what it means to be a girl or a boy?
Have you ever wondered if you might be from someplace else?

Bowie landed in an unearthly new place. A noisy jam of a rock-and-roll scene, with cranked, crunching guitars and crashing drums.

In this place, there were boys who didn't look quite like boys. Girls who didn't look quite like girls.

He transformed himself.

A new sound.

A new look.

Even a new name.

Bowie became Ziggy Stardust.

Grooving, grating guitars and drums.

Crooning, belty vocals that told Ziggy's story—an alien rockstar come to play for the people of Earth.

Ziggy's look was equally electric and fresh.

A look that defied gender.

Ziggy wore makeup, glitter, nail polish, dresses. Ziggy was affectionate with other boys. Were these things boys could do? Ziggy—and Bowie—believed they were.

Ziggy Stardust was an all-out, out-of-this-world experience—one that earned Bowie star power from worlds all over.

But pretty soon, Ziggy's story lost its sparkle, and it lost Bowie's interest. What started as a transformation now just felt normal.

It was time for Ziggy's story to come to an end.

It was time Bowie faced the change.

Soul Man

How do you describe your inside self? Your feelings, the things about you no one else knows? Can music express that part of you? Can art?

In another world, Bowie discovered a silky, smoky sound.

This was soul music.

Soul was like the sound of a beating heart. The sound of our deepest human experiences—love, sadness, hope, joy.

Bowie wrapped himself up in the smoothness of soul and its musicians.

He became the Soul Man.

His was a rich and layered sound—
velvety singers and horn players,
rhythmic, funky bass and guitar,
precise, clapping drums
and percussion.

The Soul Man was
a slinky, stick-thin gentleman.
Soft, silky vocals and backing singers,
hip, fresh sounds from talented players.

Bowie's time on planet soul was a fulfilling exploration.

But when a cold and curious darkness beckoned,
the warmth of the Soul Man began to feel too familiar.

It was time again to search for the new.

It was time he faced the change.

THE THIN WHITE DUKE

What do you do with the sadness that you feel? When you're lonely, scared, or confused? When things just don't feel right?

Not all changes are nice. Not all changes are good for you.

Bowie landed in a new place, with new sounds—cold, electronic, and clinical. In this new place, Bowie's body and mind began to suffer. He became sick, with unhealthy addictions.

He was in a deep, dark place, with deep, dark individuals.

His music and art, too, turned deep and dark.

And the Thin White Duke was born.
Beneath his familiar crooning voice were shrill and frigid sounds. Clanging, clacking electronic noise.
The Duke dressed stark in all black and white. His world was bare, lit with flashes of blinding, bright white light.

Though his art continued to flourish, the Duke shriveled and withered, trapped in a new, sick existence. He spiraled out of control.

He fell so low, so fast, it seemed as if Bowie's space exploration might come to an unfortunate end.

But when he had almost hit bottom . . .

. . . his fellow travelers caught him.

They saved him. They gave him new life.

A new purpose:

to seek something larger than ever before.

It was time he faced the change.

POP STAR

How does it feel to be appreciated and loved for your talents? What would it feel like to be loved by millions?

Bowie arrived at a new and densely populated place, where warm, catchy, feel-good music was popular. Bowie wondered . . .

How would it feel if his music were loved by the masses?

It was time for another becoming.

Bowie changed away from the strange—no more unusual looks. No more unusual sounds. He turned into what was popular—bright, bouncy, colorful suits; a bronze, sun-tanned face; and a bleach-blond blown-out brand-new hairdo.

These new songs were carefully crafted. Jingle-jangle, catchy lyrics, sugary sweet, dancey rhythm and sound,

poppy horns and keyboards,

guitar and drums,

a shiny, slick chorus of back-up singers.

Till then, Bowie had played for a single planet. The new Bowie entertained an entire solar system.

He was a bigger star than ever.

It was exactly what the people wanted. Bowie was beloved.

But in the end, what did this artist want? Who did *he* love?

Suddenly, Bowie realized, the life of a pop star, his enormous fame and popularity, forbid the creative freedom he so loved. He was loved by so many for one look, one sound, that he felt bound to stay that way.

He felt trapped by the overwhelming fame.

And so in time, he took to traveling again.

Ready again to face the change.

And on . . .
and on . . .
Bowie went.

Throughout the cosmos,
transforming,
trying on infinite different sounds,
trying out countless different looks.
And beyond.

All travels must end.

In time, we return home.

But even after Bowie's life ended,
his art lives on.

Continuously spinning,

playing,

traveling the stars . . .

beginning again

and again

and again.

Forever facing and embracing the change.

This is David Bowie.

Who are you?

BOWIE AND ME ♥

Bowie portrait from the sketchbook of Matthew Cordell

When I was seven years old, in 1983 small town South Carolina, I used my allowance to buy my very first piece of music—a single of "Modern Love" from David Bowie's album *Let's Dance*. It was catchy and cool and I played it over and over on my little record player in my bedroom, wondering about the dynamo singer pictured on the bright and colorful record sleeve. This one song would start a lifelong love in me for music—and the artists who make it.

As I grew up, my tastes changed, from pop music to rock, to punk rock, to jazz, bluegrass, world music, and beyond. It wasn't until I was in my twenties, now living in Chicago, that I came back to Bowie, when a friend was playing *Hunky Dory*, one of Bowie's earliest albums, on a cassette tape in his car. As we drove, I heard incredible songs I'd never heard before, and it inspired me to dig deeper into Bowie's long, extended catalog of music.

What struck me immediately was how different Bowie's music sounded from one album to the next. The ethereal and spacey sound of one album later changed to loud guitars and drums on another. There would be one album of soul music, another with electronic sounds, and another with catchy '80s pop music. Bowie's love for music and its countless sounds led him to many different places, much like it had with me.

Bowie's entire music career worked like that. Most musicians find a style and sound of music they like and settle in with that one sound for life. But Bowie was different. He was a true artist and an explorer—always discovering the music of other artists and finding ways to incorporate those sounds into his own music.

Bowie's approach resonated with me beyond just the music I listened to. His boundless curiosity and his eagerness to make new and different music all the time inspired me to always stay creative about the way I do things as an author and illustrator. One day, I might want to draw with a pen. Another day I'd like to paint with a brush. One day, I can tell a fictional story about a squirrel's adventure in the woods, and another, I can write about a real-life hero of mine, like Mister Rogers—or David Bowie.

Bowie's music—his art—has been an endless inspiration to me, as an artist. His music is constantly playing in my studio. He's always showing up in my sketchbook. Bowie's art and ideology is embedded in me. And now I hope he'll become part of you, too.

DAVID BOWIE THE ARTIST

David Jones was born in London in 1947 in a quiet part of town into a quiet family. But as he grew up, he realized he was different. He had a flair for the dramatic and quickly discovered interests in art and music. He began playing in bands as young as age 15, and from that time, life was quiet no more. He would go through dramatic change time and time again—the first of which was his name. There was already a popular musician named Davy Jones (of the band The Monkees), so David Jones changed his name to something less common and more edgy—David Bowie.

As Bowie set out into the world to make a life in music, he didn't know yet who he was. He first released an album in 1967 of playful music and lyrics that received little acclaim or success. Undeterred, he kept playing music, and kept thinking about what he wanted to say and how he wanted to sound. There was lots of talk about space travel in the late 1960s, with US astronauts first landing on the moon in 1969, and accordingly, Bowie was inspired to write a song with interstellar sound and lyrics. "Space Oddity" was released in the summer of 1969, and it was an immediate hit.

But with that success, Bowie wasn't simply interested in doing more of the same. The artist in him was compelled to do something different and bigger with his next project. This time, he changed his sound to hard rock, changed his name again to Ziggy Stardust, changed his gender perception, and even changed the story of his life completely. Ziggy Stardust was not human, but an alien sent to save the earth with his music.

This pattern would define David Bowie's musical career. Over and over, he traveled to new places and met new people and was inspired by all the new things he saw and heard. Over and over, the sound of the records he made changed. Bowie made a record with soulful sounds, one with electronic sounds, one with warm and catchy pop-music sounds, and on and on and over and over, changing all the time. He sometimes even ventured out into other artistic worlds, and found success as an actor, painter, and playwright. Not every Bowie album would be equally successful, but the true victory was in Bowie's determination to try new things. What tied it all together was Bowie's signature voice, and his endless drive to make surprising music for the world to hear.

Beyond his artistic life, there would be constant change too—sometimes good and sometimes bad. Marriage and divorce. Loneliness and addiction. But, ultimately Bowie would find happiness with his wife of nearly 24 years, Iman, and his children, Duncan and Lexi.

Bowie died in New York City in 2016 at the age of 69. He left behind 26 studio albums and countless other music and artistic expressions. Bowie lives on through his exceptional music and artistic legacy, through all time and space.

Always look, always listen, always stay curious to the endless incredible wonders happening all around you. You will be better and do better because of it. You will never be bored. This was the spirit of Bowie. And this is the spirit of you.

BEGINNER BOWIE PLAYLIST

If the music of David Bowie is new to you, here is a playlist of some of my personal favorites to get you started. It's a combination of hit songs and lesser-known ones from the albums released in the time frame focused on in this book (roughly 1969 to 1983). I hope you enjoy listening, and I hope that these songs inspire you to spend more time with all the incredible music created by David Bowie in his lifetime.

"Space Oddity" from *David Bowie*

There is no better way to prepare your ears and start your maiden voyage with Bowie than with his first hit single. This song sets the stage perfectly by blasting us all into space, with Bowie—as Major Tom—the captain of this most fantastic exploration.

"Changes" from *Hunky Dory*

A cleaner, simpler, early Bowie song that became permanently tied to his story as an artist. A lovely jingly-jangly song in and of itself, it's almost more important in how it touches on—even here at the beginning—the dramatic Bowie sound and visual ch-ch-changes that would define the rest of his life thereafter.

"Life on Mars?" from *Hunky Dory*

A dreamy, tinkly piano begins this waltz-like, quiet-seeming song. But it quickly erupts into an explosive, symphonic glam rock ballad with sailors, cavemen, clowns . . . oh, my! What a sound, what a scene.

"Starman" from *The Rise and Fall of Ziggy Stardust and the Spiders from Mars*

One of my personal favorites from Bowie's short stint as intergalactic superstar Ziggy Stardust. It's a catchy, singable, head-bobbing groove—complete with hand-claps and bendy guitar riffs. And the lyrics even drop on us a little hazy, cosmic Ziggy lore.

"Fascination" from *Young Americans*

This song is as rich and steamy as hot cocoa on a cold winter's day. The vibe is nice and cozy, but the complex layering of funk bass/guitar/percussion, backing singers, and brass instruments is anything but relaxed. To think that Bowie went from hard guitar rock alien to silky-smooth soul—that never doesn't blow my mind.

"Word on a Wing" from *Station to Station*

A favorite from Bowie's Thin White Duke period that perfectly captures that combination of cold and piercing electronic sounds nearly impossibly stitched together with Bowie's velvety crooning vocals. It's a strange, almost chilling packaging of feelings that somehow makes sense, brought to life immaculately by the black-and-white stick-thin Duke himself.

"Sound and Vision" from *Low*

Low is not one of Bowie's most popular albums, but it is one of my personal favorites. Lots of unusual electronic noise and sound, and the second half of the album is almost completely instrumental—no words, just music. Amidst all of this, "Sound and Vision" is a sweet, simple, bouncy tune that I really love. The electronic sounds remind me of a freshly poured tingly, tasty bubbly drink.

"Heroes" from *Heroes*

One of my all time favorite Bowie songs on another of my favorite Bowie albums. "Heroes" is a popular song on an album of songs that have a not-so-popular sound—lots of abrasive textures and instrumental exploration. It's a triumphant anthem of a song that cleverly weaves these textures into a galvanizing tapestry of unusual sounds and noises.

"It's No Game (Pt. 1)" from *Scary Monsters (And Super Creeps)*

Off the heels of his clinical sound as the Thin White Duke and beyond, Bowie kicks off this banger album and new sound with a literal scream. It opens in both Japanese and English, and Bowie's powerful belting voice is in the finest of forms. This song will grab you by the shoulders and Wake. You. Up.

"Modern Love" from *Let's Dance*

This is the song that made me a Bowie fan. The very first record I owned. I was seven years old, and Bowie lit a fire in me that's loved music and art—and the artists who make it all—ever since.

Thank you, Bowie. See you in the stars.